Paul Scott Markette

Tellwell Talent
www.tellwell.ca

ISBN
978-0-2288-3050-4 (Hardcover)
978-0-2288-3049-8 (Paperback)

For My Dad

It was a hot summer day in Beacon Falls, and Officer Greg and his K9 partner Arty were getting ready to patrol the town. Officer Greg was checking his police cruiser by turning on the lights and sirens to make sure everything was in working order.

"Woo-woo" went the siren as Officer Greg checked the siren!

The lights lit up in blue and red strobes as K9 Arty pawed at the switch.

"We are ready to Protect and Serve," exclaimed Officer Greg to Arty. "Let's go!!"

"Ruff" barked K9 Arty!

As Officer Greg and K9 Arty were pulling out of the station, Joan, the police secretary, called over the radio.

"Joan to Officer Greg, come in."

"Go ahead, this is Officer Greg and K9 Arty."

"Please see Lieutenant Eddie at Headquarters for an important assignment."

"Roger!" exclaimed Officer Greg. "We are on our way."

Officer Greg and K9 Arty quickly pulled back into police HQ and went to see Lieutenant Eddie.

"Officer Greg and K9 Arty reporting for duty, sir," exclaimed Greg as he saluted the Lieutenant.

"Ruff Ruff," barked Arty as he raised his paw to salute.

"Today is a hot summer day, and many of the townspeople will be in our parks. There is a carnival as well for the firemen in town. I want you to make sure everyone is safe so they can have fun and enjoy the day," explained the lieutenant. "Many of our officers are working today patrolling the parks and carnival," Lieutenant Eddie said. "Make sure they are safe as well."

"You can count on K9 Arty and me, sir!" shouted Officer Greg. "We won't let you down."

"Ruff Ruff," barked Arty as they both left to get started.

"Officer Tony, Officer Alicea, and Officer Kiemo are working the carnival by the firehouse. Let's go there first," Officer Greg said to K9 Arty.

As they pulled up to the firehouse, they saw several townspeople walking around carrying popcorn and cotton candy. Clowns with their faces painted and wearing silly clothing were making animal balloons for the smiling children. People were standing in line for the Ferris wheel and merry-go-round with ride tickets clutched in their hands.

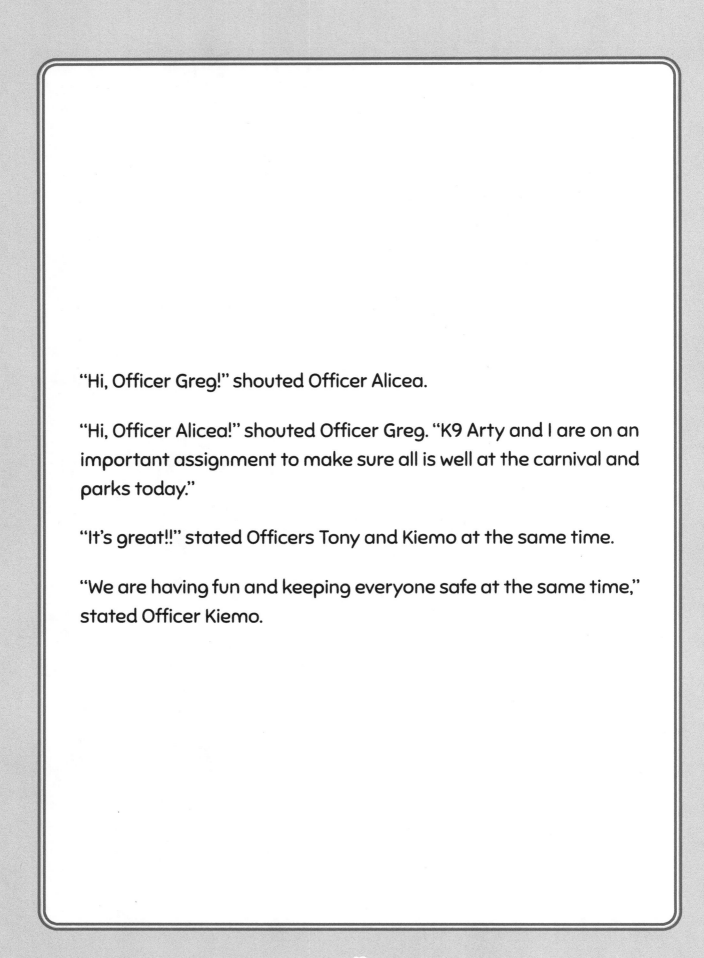

"Hi, Officer Greg!" shouted Officer Alicea.

"Hi, Officer Alicea!" shouted Officer Greg. "K9 Arty and I are on an important assignment to make sure all is well at the carnival and parks today."

"It's great!!" stated Officers Tony and Kiemo at the same time.

"We are having fun and keeping everyone safe at the same time," stated Officer Kiemo.

With that, Officer Greg and K9 Arty left for
their next destination: Mathies Park.

12

At Mathies Park, Officer Greg and K9 Arty saw several townspeople picnicking and fishing in the pond.

Officer Tim and Officer Brian were helping some of the children with their fishing lines. "Hi, Officer Greg and K9 Arty!" shouted Officer Tim.

"Want to help us put worms on these fishing lines?" asked Officer Brian.

"Anything you need, we're here to help," Officer Greg said.

"Ruff Ruff," agreed Arty.

"What a great day!!" Officer Greg said to
K9 Arty as they traveled through town.
"Where should we go next?" asked Officer Greg.

"Ruff Ruff," barked K9 Arty.

"Great idea," exclaimed Officer Greg. "Let's go to
the rec field and see which sports are being played."

"Look at all the townspeople," said Officer Greg. "They are really enjoying the beautiful summer day."

Arty stuck his head out of the window to feel the summer breeze and look at all the people in the park.

There were children playing basketball and baseball. Other people were just walking around or sitting on blankets while watching the sports activities.

"Ruff Ruff!" barked K9 Arty, pointing his nose towards two officers.

"I see Officer Jasen and Officer Rob too," Officer Greg said to K9 Arty. "Let's go check on them."

"What's the score of the game?" asked Officer Greg.

"It's a tied game in the bottom of the ninth inning," explained Officer Rob.

"I hope Beacon Falls can beat Naugatuck today," said Officer Jasen.

"We're on an important assignment from Lieutenant Eddie," said Officer Greg. "Is everything going well here?"

"It sure is!" shouted Officer Rob as a run was scored by Beacon Falls to win the game.

The crowd roared with excitement. Arty began jumping in the air and barking excitedly.

Suddenly the police radio began to stir. "Trooper Bert to Officer Greg, come in please."

"This is Officer Greg. Go ahead, Trooper Bert," said Officer Greg.

"I need you and K9 Arty to come to Toby's Pond right away. A boater has broken down in the pond and needs help," exclaimed Trooper Bert.

"We're on our way!" shouted Officer Greg. "K9 Arty, hit the lights and sirens. This is an emergency!"

Arty used his paws to hit the lights and sirens switches on, "Ruff Ruff!" barked K9 Arty and away they went!!

Officer Greg and K9 Arty arrive at Toby's Pond and speak with Trooper Bert. He explained that Mayor Gerry took his boat out in the pond and his motor failed. "Now he can't get back to shore!" screamed Trooper Bert.

"Ruff Ruff Ruff!" barked K9 Arty.

"Great idea!!" said Officer Greg. "You swim out with one end of this rope and give it to Mayor Gerry, and then Trooper Bert and I will pull you and him back to shore."

Arty, being an expert dog paddler began to swim to Mayor Gerry. Once K9 Arty reached Mayor Gerry, Mayor Gerry tied the rope to the boat. Arty then jumped into the boat with Mayor Gerry.

"Ok, pull us in," Mayor Gerry shouted to Trooper Bert and Officer Greg on shore.

"Pull...pull...pull!" shouted Officer Greg as they pulled the boat towards the shore.

"Almost there!!" screamed Trooper Bert with excitement as they pulled and pulled until the boat was ashore.

"Yayyy!" screamed the townspeople at the pond. "K9 Arty saved the mayor!! Hip hip hoorah for K9 Arty!!"

"Thank you, Officer Greg and K9 Arty. You saved the day!" cried Mayor Gerry.

K9 Arty jumped out of the boat and shook off the water from his fur. He ran to Officer Greg who was waiting for him. Officer Greg rubbed Arty's head and scratched his ears while telling him what a good boy he was. Arty's tail wagged with excitement!

"Well, Arty, another day of protecting and serving the people of Beacon Falls. You're the best partner anyone could ask for," said Officer Greg as they sat on the shore of Toby's Pond.

"Ruff Ruff Ruff," barked K9 Arty as both stared at the sunset. Arty leaned in and sat next to Officer Greg putting his head on Officer Greg's shoulder.

CPSIA information can be obtained
at www.ICGtesting.com
Printed in the USA
LVHW071751281220
675240LV00051B/1810